TAKING CARE OF YOUR

MICE AND RATS

Joyce Pope

Series consultant: Michael Findlay

Photographs by: Sally Anne Thompson
and R T Willbie/Animal Photography

Franklin Watts
New York   London   Toronto   Sydney

First Paperback Edition 1990
ISBN 0-531-15172-7

©1987 Franklin Watts
First published in Great
Britain in 1987 by
Franklin Watts
12a Golden Square
London W1

First published in the
United States of America
by
Franklin Watts Inc.
387 Park Avenue South
New York
N.Y. 10016

UK edition:
ISBN 0 86313 415 7
US edition:
ISBN 0–531–10190–6
Library of Congress
Catalog Card Number:
85–52087

Designed by
Ben White
Illustrated by
Hayward Art Group

Additional photographs
Chris Henwood 12(T),
13(T), 27(T), 28, 29(B)
Joyce Pope 7, 21(L), 23

Printed in Belgium

Acknowledgments
The photographers and publishers would like to thank
Mr Jim Rowe, Lynton Pet Shop, Gloucester; Mr Neil
Wallace, Coltham Pet Shop, Cheltenham, and the
families and their mice and rats who took part in the
photography for this book.

Special thanks are due to Chris Henwood, founder
member of the Small Mammals Genetic Circle, breeder
and adviser on rodents, for all his valuable assistance in
the preparation of this book.

TAKING CARE OF YOUR

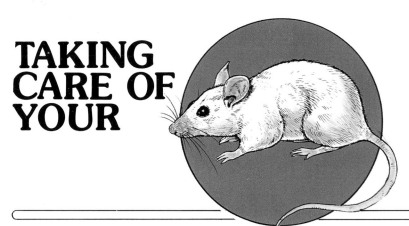

MICE AND RATS

Contents

Introduction

People like to keep pets. They can add interest to our lives. It has been proved that lonely or sick people can often be helped by the company pets can give.

By caring for and studying our pets, we can find out more about the world that both pets and people share together.

◁ Pet rats are among the most intelligent of all small animals. At one time pet rats were all white. Nowadays there are several other color varieties. This is called a "champagne rat." Rats are fun to keep because they learn all sorts of things very quickly. They are gentle and easy to handle but you must be careful never to let them escape.

Petkeepers' code

1 Remember that your pet is a living creature, not a toy.
2 Remember that your pet needs food and water every day. It must have a place where it can rest or be private, and also space in which to exercise and play.
3 Your pet depends entirely on you for its well-being, so you must be prepared to give up time for it every day, no matter how you feel.

▽ White mice are popular pets because they are cheap to buy and easy to keep. They easily become very tame.

Rats and mice belong to a big group of animals called rodents, or gnawing mammals. They all have a single pair of cutting teeth in the fronts of their mouths with which they nibble at their food.

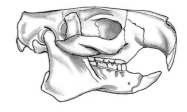

These teeth grow all through a rodent's life so pet rodents must be given something hard to nibble at or their teeth will become too long for them to feed properly.

There are many different kinds of rodents, some of which, such as

▽ Pet rats are descended from wild brown rats. They are wild and wary animals which are among the greatest of pests, destroying food and damaging buildings with their gnawing.

△ The spiny mouse is a creature from Crete and Africa. It is not as hardy as the rats and mice usually kept as pets.

△ The wood mouse is a common European animal, but it is normally active only at night, and is so alert and shy that it normally manages to avoid people. If you see one you should never try to handle it, for wild rodents can bite hard and probably will do so if they are frightened. Some carry and can pass on very unpleasant diseases, which is a good reason for leaving them alone.

gerbils, hamsters and guinea pigs, are also kept as pets. There are also many kinds of rats and mice, but most of them live only in the wild and are not kept as pets.

You may see a few quite unusual varieties of mice and rats advertised, including those pictured on this page. It is better to stick to the more common kinds as they are naturally tame and are simpler to manage.

Also, the unusual kinds may carry diseases which the more common pet mice and rats are free of.

Rats and mice make very good pets. They are inexpensive and easy to feed. They become very tame, and rats are specially interesting as they are very intelligent.

They also have two disadvantages. Their cages have to be cleaned out very frequently as mice in particular have a strong and unpleasant smell. Also, they must *never* be allowed to escape, as they are capable of breeding with wild house mice and brown rats, both of which are serious pests.

△ Since before the beginning of this century people have kept tame rats as pets. Sometimes one was born with unusual coloring, and by keeping such oddities and breeding from them, several color varieties have been developed. The one on this page is called a Black Berkshire rat.

8

Wild rats were first tamed and bred for use in laboratory experiments. Gradually people realized that they were interesting and intelligent animals and began to keep them as pets.

Most tame rats are white, with pink eyes, but many other colors are appearing, some known as hooded rats, have color on their heads, and shoulders and in a stripe along the back.

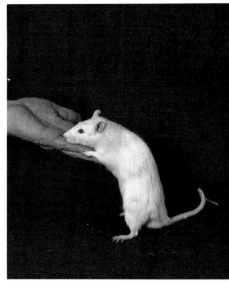

△ In earlier days many pet rats were albinos, that is to say that they were entirely white, and had pink eyes. Today some pale colored rats still have pink eyes, although hooded rats, which are only partly white, do not.

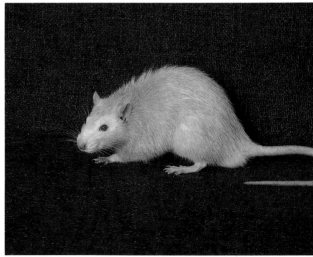

△ A silver fawn rat with red eyes.

◁ A brown-hooded rat with dark eyes.

Tame mice were also first used as laboratory animals. There are now more than 40 varieties with different colored coats. Some mice are long-haired and others are curly-coated.

▷ A mouse with brown pigments, like this parti-colored mouse, has brown eyes.

▽ An albino mouse has no color pigment in its body so its fur is always white. Albinos have red or pink eyes, because the color of their blood shows through.

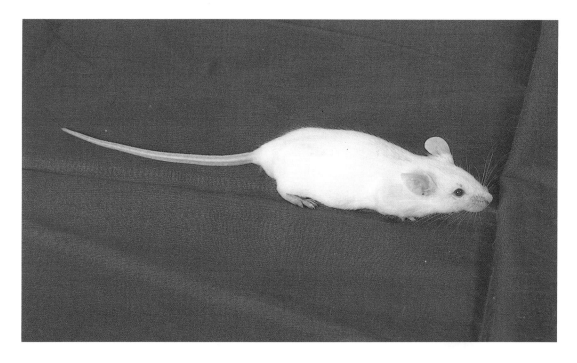

△ A grey and white parti-colored mouse is known as a mis-marked Dutch mouse.

▷ This pale golden colored mouse is called a fawn variety.

When you have permission to keep a pet rat or mouse, you must prepare a place for it to live in.

You will need a cage made of strong plastic or metal, as rats and mice can gnaw through anything else. Find a suitable place for it, which is warm, but not in direct sunlight. It should also be away from drafts and open windows.

△ Here are 3 different kinds of cages, including a stacking cage. These are very good, but they are expensive. Your pets will always enjoy the chance to explore and play outside their cage.

◁ This is a good ready-made cage to keep mice in. It has good sleeping quarters and a solid backed wheel for exercise.

There are many types of cages, but it must be large enough to give your pet plenty of room for exercise. Mice are very good climbers, so if you do not have a great deal of space, you can make a tall cage, with several floors with ladders between them that the mice can climb. There should be a dark sleeping place – a box with a hole cut in one side or even a flower pot will do.

It should also have an exercise wheel with a solid back, like the one shown in the picture. Get suitable containers for food and water; enough dry food for the first week; peat or wood chips (not sawdust) for floor covering and bedding material.

△ A piece of pipe makes a hiding place and a toy for pet rats and mice.

▽ A home-made rat cage like this is fine, but the rat will need to be taken out for exercise and play.

13

Be sure any female mouse or rat you buy has not been in a cage with a male for at least three weeks, or you may suddenly find a large number of baby rats or mice at home.

Never keep both males and females in the same cage, as they breed very rapidly. You would then find it difficult to get rid of all their young.

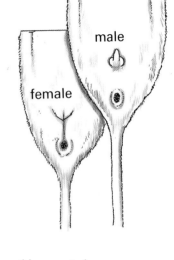

◁ In a pet shop you can see lots of color varieties of mice, and you can choose the ones that you like best. It is better to get two female mice – two males would fight.

It is best to keep two female mice as they like the company of their own kind. If you are sure that you will have lots of time to play with it, you could keep one rat on its own but, in general, it is better to have two. Unlike most other animals, two male rats will live happily together and they make better pets than females.

You should choose young animals: mice about four weeks old, rats not more than six weeks. Pick the animals with bright eyes and shiny coats. Do not take any that are sneezing or have runny noses. Make sure that the droppings in their cage are dark-colored and firm; this also is a sign of good health.

△ You will need to have a secure warm box in which to carry your new pet home – you can probably get one from the pet shop, but you should check this first.

◁ Always choose a healthy looking animal. One that has bright eyes and glossy fur is likely to be well and strong. It is also a good sign if it is active and taking an interest in things.

Your new pets at home

Carry your new pets home as quickly and as gently as possible and put them into the cage that you have prepared. Mice will soon discover their own dark sleeping place and may stay there for a while.

Rats will usually explore their living space quite quickly and then settle down to feed or groom themselves.

Both mice and rats will usually

▷ Your pet will quickly learn to recognize you. To make it tame you must be quiet and gentle, so as not to frighten it. This rat is ready to leap away, but its curiosity is overcoming its fear. Soon it will be quite tame and confident.

◁ You can encourage your pet with a special tidbit, such as a sunflower seed.

settle into their new homes very soon. Then you can begin to make them tame.

You must move very slowly and let the animal come to you. Offer it a tidbit, such as a sunflower seed, and curiosity will soon overcome your pet's fear.

When the animal takes food from you willingly, try picking it up. Hold a rat two-handed; one hand over its back, the other slipped under its tummy to support the weight. When it feels more confident and fairly sure that you will not hurt it, the rat will walk onto your hand without hesitation.

△ You may want to pick your mouse up once it is really tame. Do so as shown here, holding it near the base of the tail – *never* hold the tip of the tail.

Wild rats and mice will eat almost anything that human beings eat. However, your pets will need special food. It is best to give them two meals a day. You can buy commercial mouse or rat food, or "rodent chow." This should be fed in the morning.

In the early evening, give them more of the mixture, but add some tidbits, such as a little wholewheat bread, moistened with milk, and

▷ The food bowls should be heavy so that a rat or mouse cannot tip them over, or drag them about. An earthenware bowl like this one is ideal. It is also easy to clean.

◁ Rats and mice often take food from their bowls and eat it in a corner of the cage. They can use their front paws like hands to hold nuts or such pieces of food.

some nuts or a piece of dried fruit.

Rats enjoy pieces of hard boiled egg, scraps of bacon rind or even a small piece of bone to gnaw at. The amount of food you give depends on the size of the animals. Don't overfeed as uneaten food must be thrown away each time the cage is cleaned.

As well as dry food, pet rats and mice need some fresh vegetables or fruit. You can give them small pieces of food that you don't eat, such as apple cores, or the tops of carrots or beetroots.

Finally, always check that your pets have fresh water. It is best to use a water bottle with a "sipper tube" so that the water will not become fouled. Your pets will soon learn how to drink from it.

▽ Rats and mice need a varied diet including fresh vegetables to keep them healthy, like this rat. They sometimes make a hoard of all of the food that you give them. This rat is removing a piece of carrot to put in its own private corner.

Toys for your pets

A living place, empty except for their sleeping quarters, would be very dull for mice and rats and might even cause them to gnaw at their cage in boredom.

Both animals need something hard to nibble on. Your pet store may sell blocks of hardwood which are suitable for this purpose. If you can find a small piece of hardwood from a fruit tree for example, this will do just as well as a bought one.

▷ Your pet will spend most of its time in its cage, so you must give it toys to add variety to its life. A piece of tube – either cardboard from a paper roll, or small sized plastic drain pipe makes a good place for exploration and play.

△ When it comes out of its cage, a rat or mouse likes to explore you, especially if it knows that you are likely to have a tidbit hidden in your pocket.

△ Your pet needs something hard to gnaw to keep its teeth in trim. A big piece of hardwood like this is fine to climb and play on, as well as to chew.

A wheel with a solid back which prevents damage to tails gives good exercise, as do ladders and twigs wedged into the cage. Rats are not quite so agile as mice, so they need more solid branches to climb.

Both animals enjoy having a short length of pipe that they can squeeze themselves through. Many rats are hoarders; they like to collect and hide all sorts of things – candy wrappers, acorns or pieces of carrot may all be added to their pile of hidden treasures. Try giving them a range of small objects, to see which they prefer. Don't include anything made of brittle plastic which could injure the animal.

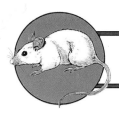
Mice and rats are active animals, particularly in the evening. When you are quite sure that they are tame enough, they can be allowed out of their cage. Make sure that no other pets, especially cats or dogs, are allowed in the same room at the time. They would normally kill mice or rats, given a chance to do so.

Don't let mice loose on the floor,

▽ The best way for your pet to get exercise in its cage is with an exercise wheel. Ideally it should be attached to the wall of the cage and have a solid back, like this one. This prevents the animal's tail from being trapped or damaged.

as they may squeeze into a small place from which you cannot remove them.

Rats love to explore. You can make a game for them by building a maze of books on a table top and hiding food at the end of it.

Never leave a mouse or rat alone while it is playing outside its cage. They are very nosey and this can make them very destructive.

△ When your rats or mice are completely tame you can let them play outside their cage. You must be sure that there are no dogs or cats around, and that the doors and windows are closed.

Rats are very agile and can climb very well. You must watch them when they are exploring, or they may damage your toys or books. They can be very destructive if left on their own.

◁ Mice and rats groom every part of themselves every day, using their paws to comb their fur. This rat is nibbling at toes on one of its hind feet to clean them.

You will have to pay close attention to keeping the cages clean. Every day you should remove any droppings, which are usually deposited in one part of the cage. You can buy sterile mouse-and-rat bedding at your pet store. Second best would be a thick layer of wood chips or shredded newspaper. This absorbs the smell, but with mice you will probably find that it still needs to be renewed once a week – or even more often.

Rats smell much less, but even so, their floor litter should be replaced

◁ Mice and rats use their forepaws to wash their faces. They often then turn round and run their tails through their hands to clean them of any bits of grit or other dirt. They may lick and nibble their tails as well

frequently. You will also need to "spring clean" your pet mouse's or rat's cage fairly frequently. It is useful to have a temporary cage for your pets while you scrub and disinfect their main home, as this must be completely dry before you return the animals to it.

The floor litter should be replaced entirely, but you should keep a little of the old bedding to put in the sleeping quarters. This will have a familiar smell and will reassure your pets when they go back to their usual home.

△ Apart from the routine of cage cleaning, you must remember to wash your pets' food bowls in very hot water every day. Unlike their wild relatives, tame mice and rats should not have any diseases that you can catch. Even so, you should wash your hands whenever you have been playing with them or caring for them.

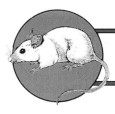

Mouse and rat health

If a mouse or rat shows definite signs of illness, it may be too late for a cure. However, if they are well kept, mice may live for over 2 years, and rats for up to 5 years without suffering from any diseases at all.

▷ This rat's claws have grown too long so the vet is trimming them back.

▽ Check your pets' teeth and claws quite often to make sure that they have not grown too long.

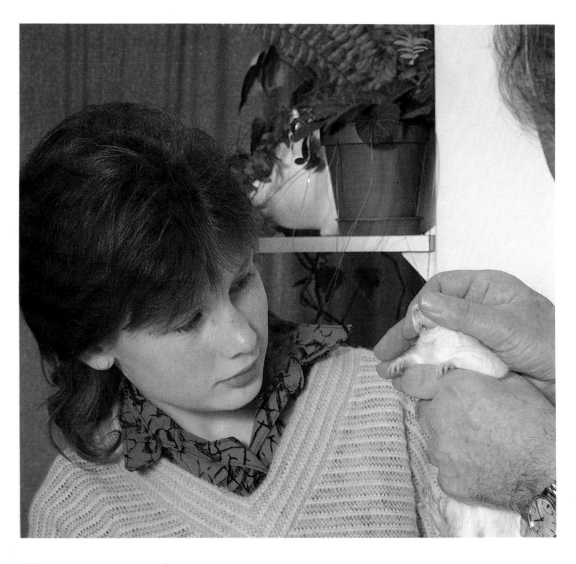

A sick mouse or rat is generally listless, has a dull coat and will probably not want to eat. One reason for the loss of appetite may be that the animal's front (incisor) teeth have grown too long. Visit your local veterinarian who will be able to clip them back to the right length. Give your pet suitable hard toys to gnaw and this trouble should be prevented.

Mice and rats are very sensitive to changes in temperature. You must be careful in finding the right place for their cages. Drafts and dampness can cause bronchitis or pneumonia, which can be fatal.

▽ This mouse has been bitten and needs to be moved to another cage to be bathed with a mild antiseptic.

If you look after your pets properly, you are bound to watch them, to discover how they live and what they like and dislike. You can find out a great deal about them by planning your observations and putting them in a pet project book.

For example, measure how fast your pet mouse or rat grows. Weigh

▽ You can make a very interesting pet project book which can include dates when you noted things about your pet, photographs and drawings.

it, measure the length of one of its hind feet and the length of its tail. Does the tail grow much longer as the mouse or rat grows older?

Find out what sort of food your rat prefers. Hide a nut or a sunflower seed and a piece of bacon or carrot near to each other. See which is taken first. Does the rat always make the same choice? Try putting small amounts of its favorite food in different-colored bowls. See whether it prefers one color to another.

△ If you know somebody who breeds rats or mice you can watch the development of the babies. Notice how fast they grow, and also how their mother cares for them and is prepared to defend them.

◁ Weigh and measure your mouse to see how fast it grows but be careful that it does not escape.

Checklist

 Before you buy:

1 Make sure that you have your parents' permission and that there is somewhere suitable to keep your pets.
2 Get a cage, floor litter and bedding.
3 Get food and water dishes, and a supply of food.

 Daily:

1 Clean out droppings and remove uneaten green food.
2 Wash food bowls (separately from the family's dishes).
3 Check that there is enough water in the container.
4 Feed your pets in the morning and late afternoon.
5 Play with your pets.

 Weekly:

1 Scrub and disinfect the cage. Use 30ml(1oz) chlorine bleach to 1l(1qt) of water.
2 Replace floor-litter (wood shavings, etc.) and most of bedding for all mice and rats.
3 Wash and refill water-container.
4 Check that your pets have not been gnawing their cage. If they have, repair it.
5 Check and, if necessary, replace branches and any other toys that have been badly chewed.

 Occasionally:

1 Check teeth and claws to make sure that they have not grown too long.

Questions and answers

Q What is the scientific name of my pet mouse?
A *Mus musculus*

Q What is the scientific name of a pet rat?
A *Rattus norvegicus*

Q What size cage do I need to keep a mouse?
A At least 60cm(24in) × 30cm(12in) × 30cm(12in).

Q What size cage do I need to keep a pet rat?
A At least 76cm(30in) × 30cm(12in) × 30cm(12in).

Q Can cats and dogs become friends with rats and mice?
A It is possible, but not very likely. It is much safer not to have a cat or a dog in the room when your mice or rats are outside their cage.

Q Can I keep a mouse and a rat together?
A Rats and mice do not get along well together and should always be kept separately.

Q Can I keep two mice (or rats) of different colors together?
A Yes. The fur color makes no difference.

Q Is it fair to keep a rat (or mouse) on its own?
A They tend to be very social animals so it's kinder to keep two males or two females together, **not** a male and a female.

Index